Coming Out Of The Rain

By

Pastor Charles C. Brown

This book is a work of fiction. Places, events, and situations in this story are purely fictional. Any resemblance to actual persons, living or dead, is coincidental.

© 2002 by Pastor Charles C. Brown. All rights reserved.

No part of this book may be reproduced, stored in a retrieval system, or transmitted by any means, electronic, mechanical, photocopying, recording, or otherwise, without written permission from the author.

ISBN: 1-4033-1642-2

This book is printed on acid free paper.

1st Books - rev. 06/19/02

Acknowledgments.

First and foremost I would like to thank God for the storms of life that made me better. To my wife the woman that completes me, and has supported me from the beginning I will always love you. Latasha this one is for you. To my beautiful mother Bernice Brown, and to my supportive father Solomon Brown when everyone laughed and told me to give up it was the both of you that encouraged me to run this race. To my son Charles Clifford Brown Jr. the greatest son in the world you are a special part of me. To my wonderful daughter Tresyah who could ask for anything more always remember how important you both are in my life. To Gregory,

Deborah, Patrick, Patricia, and Joy through all of our ups and downs we've always been there for each other. Luv ya. To My granny Earnestine Howard thank you for all of your years of wisdom. To the heart of Mississippi my beautiful mother-in-law Ms. Naomi Little I see where Bird gets it from. Much love. To my New Heaven Christian Church family, the little church with the big heart, thank you for hanging in there with me. I truly love you all. Were going places!!! To the original Sportmart posse, Patrick, Greg, Big John, Aaron, Latricia, Katrina, Maryland, Yolanda, Lil Charles, Tammy, Charnett, and Cortney much love. To my LaSalle family Molly, Greg, Marva, Otillia, Tracy, Lucy, Patty, Ms. Vonda, Mrs. Fields, Ms. Amato, and Kathy I love you all. To some of the greatest preachers this side of Heaven Pastor A.R. Williams, Pastor L. Banks, Pastor J.M. Williams. Pastor X. Williams, Pastor J. Davis, my right hand man Rev Anton Godfrey, Pastor J. Collins, Pastor W.J. Campbell, Pastor Cooley, and Pastor F. Martin thank you all for your guidance and support through out the years. To Creation Community Choir you showed me that real men do praise God. To Bethlehem Unity M.B.C my home away from home, to New St. Matthew M.B.C, Great True Vine M.B.C, Mountain Top M.B.C, and to St. James COGIC thank you for the many seeds that you have sown in my spirit. To Jalon Jaddua (You thought I forgot about you) stay on the ship. To my aunts, uncles, nephews, nieces, cousins, sister-in-laws, brother-in-laws, friends, and to everyone else that I missed I love you all. To Jay and Quan a special blessing I give to you, I pray that your marriage is blessed, and that God will give unto you all the things that your hearts desire. Peace.

CONTENTS

Acknowledgments. iii

Introduction. ix

1. Understanding The Rain. 1

2. Experiencing the Rain.. 19

3. Dressing For The Weather................................. 33

4. No Signs Of Letting Up..................................... 50

5. Standing Alone In The Strom. 65

6. A Leaky Roof. 79

7. Taking Charge of the Storm. 103

8. Showers of The Anointing: A New Beginning... 128

INTRODUCTION.

There are only a few things in life that we can be sure of, and one of these things is the fact that we shall all have our fair share of storms. Some storms shall be fierce, while others may seem mild. Some storms shall be expected, and others will be totally unexpected. Winds will blow, breakers will dash, clouds will roll in, and it will rain. There is no doubt about it storms will come, but they shall not last always.

Now you must understand that the importance of the storm is not found in how the storm handles you, but it's in how you handle the storm. There are important principles to be found in every aspect of the storm, and in this book you will learn how to apply these principle to overcoming your situations. A storm by definition is any commotion or agitation that disrupts the norm, and in this book you will learn how to calm these agitations. And in those few instances that you will not be able to calm the raging winds, you will learn how to ride them into higher grounds.

There was a time in my life when it seemed as though every other day it was one storm after another. My life seemed hopeless, and I felt like nothing mattered. Like a little rag doll I was tossed from wave to wave. I didn't know how to fight, or how to overcome my storms. All I knew was that my boat of life was taking on water, and I was sinking quickly. It was not until I had made up my mind to get a handle on my situation did I begin to come out of the storm.

I began to understand the rain, and through my understanding came strength. I began to experience the rain, and from these experiences I found my will to live again. I learned how to dress for the weather, which prepared me for anything. Even when there were no signs of letting up I learned how to trust in the Lord in spite of my situations. When I was standing all-alone in the storm, I found out who I really was, and what I really wanted. When my roof was leaking, I learned the foundational concepts of love, trust, communication, and commitment. I learned how to take charge of my storm, I was showered with the anointing, and I found a new beginning, and this is what I share with you. The enemy was defeated when he allowed you to pick up this book, for from this moment on <u>YOU ARE COMING OUT OF THE RAIN</u>.

Chapter 1

Understanding The Rain.

As the rain falls, the solitary drops begin to dance across the rooftops. Then they slowly and meticulously begin to cascade down the windowsills. These soft, soothing, and somewhat rhythmic sounds can be a very relaxing sedative. Young lovers cuddle closely together, while walking hand and hand in a warm cozy embrace. And as their umbrellas shelter them from the cool summers rain, they longingly and lovingly make plans for their future lives together. The roses so soft and sweet open wide their brightly colored lips, and drink in this life giving nectar as it falls from the skies above. The rain is known to have magical and mystical effects upon the world.

But what happens when the rain does not stop, and the drizzle becomes a storm? What happens when the floods come, and our dreams are washed away in a stream of desperation? What happens when it rains so hard that the basements of our emotions begin to flood? Where do we run to when the bridges of life are washed away, and carried down stream on a raging river of loneliness?

For some of us our lives seem to be one big rainstorm after another. Many of us feel as though in our lives the rain will never end. It just keeps coming and coming, wave after wave, like a never-ending vicious cycle. Deep within the very depths of our souls many of us have a feeling that if we can just reach a level of dryness, or somehow make it to higher ground everything will be all right. If we can just reach a level in our lives, where the rain will stop falling maybe just maybe this life will make more sense.

While on the other hand there are some of us, who have actually taken up refuge in the storm. They have used the rain to hide their tears, and to wash away their grief? This is the tribe that I once belonged to. My life had been filled with so much pain, and sadness that the only place that I could find refugee in was in the midst of the storm. The only place that I found peace was in the rain.

I wandered aimlessly throughout the downpour, refusing to carry an umbrella, for I felt that in the rain no one could see the tears that were in my eyes. No one could see the badge of sorrow that I wore around my neck, like a medal of honor given to a fallen solider. I had reached a level in my life, where I felt as though things could never get any better. At times it can rain so hard that you begin to feel as though you will never embrace the warm sunshine again. And instead of looking for a way out, you begin to find a sense of belonging in the storm.

Coming Out of the Rain

But when you give in to this spirit of despair, the only thing that you are doing is admitting defeat. If you ever want the rain to stop, you must first realize that the rain serves a unique purpose in your life. Then you must begin to realize that no matter who you are in your life it will rain sometime. The Lord allows it to rain in your life for a reason, for there is a remarkable lesson to be learned in the midst of the storm. He has to show you that in spite of what you are going through He is still in control. That no matter the problem, or the circumstance that you may be dealing with the Creator of the heavens, and the ends of the earth is yet able to see you through. It will rain in your life, my life, and in everyone else

Charles C. Brown

...that lives upon God's green earth because the Lord has no respect of person, and his word tells us so in the book of Matthew 5:45:

For he maketh his sun to rise on the evil and on the good, and sendeth rain on the just and on the unjust.

Accepting the rain for what it is begins the healing process. My wounds did not begin to heal until I began to realize that the rain had an objective, and it was not to hide my pain, but to wash it away. I began to understand that while I was yet walking in the rain I was being refreshed and rejuvenated.

That may sound strange to some because many of us cannot fathom a storm of life as a rejuvenator.

But believe it or not rain builds character, and gives depth to ones soul. This is the reason why it is so extremely important that you pick up this spirit, or frame of mind because when you do so in actuality what you're doing is opening the door to a whole new world of opportunities. You are actually allowing your storm to pass by quicker, and it also gives you a higher level of understanding. You begin to look at the storm as being just a little rain. You begin to realize that problems in your marriage, in your home, in your finances, and on your job are just a little rain. And not only is it just a little rain, but this to shall pass for it cannot rain always.

You must take comfort in knowing that during the days of Noah it rained for forty days and forty nights, but one day it had to stop. It had to stop because of the divine order of God, and because of His master plan. God knew it would rain in your life. He knew when, He knew where, and He also knew for how long. He knew exactly how much rain you could bear, so He allowed it to rain just enough for you to receive the predetermined lesson that He had planned for you from the very beginning of time. Only after learning your lesson will the rain stop, and the rain must stop because in spite of it all the hands of the Master are yet at work, for the Apostle Paul said in Romans 8:29:

For whom he (the Lord) did foreknow, he also did predestinate to be conformed to the image of his son.

It cannot, shall not, and will not rain all the time. It shall only rain until God says, "That's enough," and then it shall cease. Then the sun shall shine, the birds shall sing, and a rainbow shall appear across the sky as a sign to let you know that the Lord is still with you, and that His promises endure forever.

Now, I do realize that there will be times when we can become blinded by the falling rain, but that is the perfect opportunity to begin to develop the ability to see through the storm. There is a calmness that lies within the midst of the storm that you must begin to focus upon, for within the very heart of the storm is where the winds will stop blowing, and the rain will stop falling. There is a place in the heart of the storm that no matter what is going on around you, you still have peace.

That is the level in which you must strive to achieve. You must make it to the level in the storm, where you can say, "No matter how bad the storm may seem I still have joy." When you reach that level, you can make it no matter what is going on in your life. When my life was at it's lowest level, and it seemed as though everything was going wrong I made a decision to weather the storm. When all of my so-called friends had left me to fend for myself, and I had no one else to turn to that is when I made a consciences decision to make it through. That is when I decided that if I've got to struggle and fight on my own in order to make it than so be it, for without a shadow of a doubt I must make it into the eye of the storm.

When it began to rain in my life, it started out as cool as a spring rain on a hot summers day. But before long the storm was as fierce as Hurricane Devastation destroying everything in its path. It was a time in my life when I had to stand up for what I believed in. And it seemed to me, when a man stands up for his principles everything should fall into place. I mean after all should not right follow right? At least that is what we are taught.

But what I had failed to realize, was that the first sign of rain was a warning signal that a storm maybe heading my way. Those first sprinkles of raindrops that I felt upon my face were signs that something bigger maybe coming. At times I could smell the rain in the air, I could see the clouds rolling in, and those were my warning signs. That was the time to close the window, bring in the wash from off the line, and prepare the storm shelter. That was the time to prepare myself for the worst.

I mean I saw the skies darkening, I felt the rain falling, I heard the thunder roaring, and I saw the lightening flashing. I knew that a storm was on the way, but I did not take heed to it. One of the worst things that you can do is allow a storm to catch you off guard. The one who is unprepared for a storm is the one that is prepared to be devastated. But glory be to God, for although I was unprepared for the storm, the storm had been prepared for me.

There is a level in life that the Lord our God wants you to achieve. So when He is ready for you to receive that which He has in store for you, He sets His plan for your life into motion. Now you must understand that by no means will He force you to accept your destiny, but He will allow the storm to rage uncontrollably in your life until you finally begin to realize that if you do not accept your predetermined level in life the rain may never cease.

I had to learn my lesson the hard way. I can remember a time when it seemed as though everywhere I turned I would run into a brick wall. I was like a man walking forward on a moving sidewalk that was stuck in reverse. I was empty on the inside. I felt as though my life had no value, and regardless of who or what was around me something was still missing. My life was incomplete. I can still hear that familiar phrase that I would often recite echoing over and over in the archives of my mind. Far too often I found myself saying, "There is something that I am not doing, and until I find out what that something is my life will never be complete." And in my search for that feeling of completeness I tried everything that I could think of in order to obtain that sense of wholeness, but the one major point that I was not realizing was the fact that if the ability to make myself feel complete was in my possession I would have done so long ago.

In my feeble attempt to find myself I lost my vision, my direction, and my purpose for life, and one of the most vital aspects in overcoming a storm is the ability to maintain your vision. You must have some sense of where you're going, and where you want to be. Some people walk aimlessly through out life, and never accomplish anything because they have no vision. They have no idea of self purpose, and or destiny, and the word of God teaches us in the book of Proverbs 29:18:

Where there is no vision, the people perish:

You must embrace your time of storm as a period of readjustment, and as a time to reexamine your situations. You must begin to look past the rain, and find the source of your pain.

Your time of readjustment is a time to search for wisdom and understanding. These two concepts go hand and hand, with one complimenting the other. That is why the word of God says in the book of Proverbs 4:7:

Wisdom is the principal thing; therefore get wisdom: and with all thy getting get understanding.

You must understand that the rain does serve a purpose, and that purpose is to give you power.

Many times the intensity of the storm will act as a driving force that pushes you back into the pathway that was meant for you to travel in the beginning. While other times that same storm is meant to push you out of your level of comfort, and into a higher level of spirituality. Causing you to go against the grain, and to move out into uncharted waters.

This is where wisdom and understanding come into play, for you must know the difference between the two. You must be able to determine the type of storm that you are in, so that you will be able to handle yourself accordingly. Wisdom tells you what to do, and understanding tells you how to do it.

Once you have the what, and the how in the right order the application becomes second nature. Then you will begin to maneuver through your storm, like the captain of your destiny cutting through the Antarctic's of life, with the greatest of easy, and it all begins with understanding the storm.

Chapter 2

Experiencing the Rain.

While we are yet in the midst of the storm, we must begin to realize that no matter how hopeless our lives may seem we are all born with an in depth desire to live. We all possess an inner spirit that acts as a driving force compelling us to experience this life to the fullest. We want to examine, absorb, and explore everything that life has to offer. Watching a child experience the joys of life for the very first time is a wonderful, and spiritually uplifting phenomenon. Watching their facial expressions, and seeing their eyes light up when they're introduced to a new sensation is awe inspiring to say the least.

But what happens between the wonder years, and adulthood that causes life's encounters to become mundane? What is that one thing that takes away our desire to live this life to the highest level? Many of us believe that after you've reached a certain age you have experienced everything that this life has to offer. We often say, "Life's experiences are no longer new, but simply routine." Many of us have deposited this ideology within our spirits, and it has bloomed into a self-destroying sense of been there, and done that.

Now it is my personal belief that life's experiences can never become routine, nor could we ever experience everything that this life has to offer. But in actuality what we have done is allowed the experiences of life to change the way in which we view how our lives should be lead, and in doing so we have allowed these experiences to smolder out the candle sticks of life that were intended to brighten our paths.

Many of us may not realize this, but our past experiences prepare us for our future reactions. In other words how we experience life today, has a great deal of influence on how we will live our lives tomorrow. Many of us have had to deal with situations in our lives that have caused us to fall short of our primary goals. Many of us have had experiences in our lives that have been so detrimental, that they have caused us to say, "No matter what I do, it always ends in the same way."

We will even go as far as to say, "Why should I even try to do anything different, when I already know exactly how everything is going to turn out?" But what you must begin to realize is that is does not matter what the situation may be, and it does not matter how similar a situation may look each circumstance is different. And therefore we must handle each experience with a different approach, and with a different frame of mind.

Just because a particular incident ended in one way in the past in no way does that determine how it will end in the future. Life's experiences are to be examined, learned from, and then released. Holding on to the lesson, while letting go of the episode. Because if we do not let go we will carry around dead luggage, and not only will the luggage weigh us done, but it will also keep us from reaching our goals.

Many of us are carrying around great deals of excess baggage in our spirits that we have accumulated over the years, and this baggage is causing a great strain on our spiritual growth. We can not bring old luggage into a new house, and the word of God teaches us this very same concept in the book of Matthew 8:16:

No man putteth a piece of new cloth unto an old garment, for that which is put in to fill it up taketh from the garment, and the rent (tear) is made worst.

In other words it's time to let go. The time has come for us to let the old things die, and to let the past stay in the past. You cannot let who you were, or what you may have done determine what you will be. Instead of building on old hurts and pains the time has come for us to totally demolish those old hindrances, and begin to build on a clean slate.

It is time to take charge of our lives, examine our situations, and find the causes of our dilemmas. We must begin to ask ourselves the right questions. We must begin to find out who, what, when, and how. How did I get here, what steps did I take, and what decisions did I make that caused me to be at this point in my life? We must begin to take on the responsibilities for our own actions. We must begin to realize that examining our situations causes us to stop, and take a closer look at the bigger picture. Not only must we examine our situations, but we must also be ready to make some major changes in our lives. In many of our cases we will find that we are the biggest cause for the majority of our problems, and not only that, we will also find that for the majority of the time we are our own worst enemies.

In our time of self-examination we must steal away into a place of seclusion, and serenity in order to get in touch with who we truly are. We have learned in the word of God in the book of Psalms 91:1:

He that dwelleth in the secret place of the Most High shall abide under the shadow of the almighty.

Far too often we never receive the right answers that we are so diligently searching for because our lives are being bombarded with far too many outside forces. These forces or spirits are acting as negative energy siphons sapping us of our positive energy, and draining us of our spiritual potency. These forces can be our friends, family, careers, and even fellow church members. These negative forces are anything, and anyone that can hinder us from getting to the level of peace in the Lord that it takes for us to hear from him. These forces are extremely cunning, and they realize that in order for us to receive the answers that so many of us are diligently searching for we must reach this level of tranquility, and they're job is to try to do anything and everything to stop us from making it. But your job is to do anything and everything that it takes to make it, and to ensure that you hear from the Lord.

Pastor Charles C. Brown

I can remember times in my life, when I felt like a ship without a sail aimlessly drifting down the rivers of life. I had no direction, and I had no focus. And although I wanted to get better, and I truly desired to find the purpose for my life somehow I just could not. It seemed as though no matter how hard I tried to capture the purpose for my life somehow it continued to elude me, and to slip through my fingertips. And the worst part of it all was the fact that the majority of the people that were around me at that crucial time in my life inside of building me up, they were tearing me down. Instead of giving me some type of positive reinforcement they chose to bring out the negative aspects, and in doing so they were spiritually assassinating me.

When I needed words of encouragement that would help me, I received words of destruction that were hindering me. People would make comments such as, "You must have done something to deserve what you are getting." "There must be a problem with your salvation." "You might as well accept it because this is as good as life will ever get." "You shouldn't aim so high, you know where you are from, you know where you are at, and you know that your life will never get any better."

Each and every word was like a dagger plunging deep within the very depths of my dying soul.

Stabbing me over, and over, and over again until I was as the walking dead. It was not until I got by myself, and talked to myself about myself, that I started to get my life back on the right track.

I have found that the importance of down time, or time spent in self-examination cannot be underestimated because it allows you to take a closer look at yourself, without the help or influences of others. It allows us to strip off our mask, and to remove the make-up that we much too often don when we are in the presence of others. It allows us to look past the shallow grins, and hollow smiles that we tend to hide behind.

Self-examination allows us to look past the strong exterior walls, and barriers that we have erected in order to protect our feelings. The walls that we believe will show the world that nothing can in no way harm us, or move us out of our level of comfort. Self examination gives us the time, and the opportunity to be truthful with ourselves, for the word of God tells us in 2 Corinthians 13:5:

Examine yourselves, whether ye be in the faith; prove your own selves.

You must begin to look inside of yourself, and in spite of your situation pull out the person that God wants you to be. You cannot allow the devil to steal this important time away from you. There is a

Pastor Charles C. Brown

mighty man or woman of God that lives deep within us all that is truly desiring to be set free, and in your times of self-examination that freedom can be achieved.

Chapter 3

Dressing For The Weather.

I can remember when I was younger, and the weatherman would make an announcement that, "It was going to rain." Before I left the house the very first thing that my mother would tell me was, "Don't forget your umbrella." She wanted to make sure that I was protected from the elements. She wanted me to be prepared for whatever Mother Nature had in store. She would cover me from head to toe, with the latest in rain apparel. When the other children would arrive at school drenched from the sudden cloud burst, I would arrive high and dry, and ready for an experience in higher learning.

Now I can also remember times when although the forecast would call for rain there would not be a cloud in the sky. But there I was this little rubber coated boy on my way to school all ready for Hurricane Andrew, and not even a sprinkle would I receive. Nevertheless, I can still hear those magical words that Mother Brown would ever so often recite unto me. Time and time again she would say, "It is better to have an umbrella and not need it. Then to need an umbrella and not have it."

In a nutshell what she was saying to me was that it is always best to be prepared, for preparation is the key to withstanding a storm. Being prepared for a storm is simply allowing yourself to acquire a spiritually open frame of mind that is accessible unto the will of God. This in turn will give you an inner foresight, or a spiritual guide light that will lead you out of even the roughest of storms.

Through out our lives we are often drilled on being prepared. In preparation for our futures we are told to get a good education. In order to be prepared for the jobs of tomorrow we are often told to make a start today. Before a big fight a professional boxer will spend months in preparation, and training for his up and coming bout. Before a big case a lawyer will spend hours and hours deliberating over case files, and combing through evidence. In every aspect of life anyone that plans to succeed must first be prepared for the task that is at hand, and weathering a storm is no different.

And now the question that is laid upon the table is, how do you prepare yourself for a storm? And the answer is, you must dress for the weather. And your dress code is found in the word of God in Ephesians 6:11 were the Apostle Paul said:

Put on the whole armor of God, that ye may be able to stand against the wiles (snares) of the devil.

Having on the whole armor of God allows you to tackle the storm under the leadership, direction, and authority of a much higher power. Putting on the armor of God not only gives you fighting power, but it allows you to yield unto His will. Which in fact guarantees you the victory, for the Lord our God promised you in the book of Zechariah 4:6 that the victory is yours and it's:

Not by might, nor by power, but by my spirit, saith the Lord of hosts.

Putting on the Lord's armor submits you to his authority, which in turn opens up the avenue to your deliverance. When you submit yourselves unto the will of God in actuality what you are saying is, "This storm is far to much for me, and I can not fight it on my own." What you are doing is telling the Lord that, "I have tried to weather this storm under my own power, and instead of getting better I've gotten worst. So now Lord I'm turning it over to you, for this battle is yours."

This was not the easiest lesson for me to learn. I can recall many times in my life where I charged off into battle without being prepared to fight. And when I think back to how those very same battles that raged on uncontrollable for what seemed like months or years could have been won in a matter of days or hours, if I had only been prepared.

Now preparation, or dressing for success much like anything else of major importance comes in steps, and these steps are outlined in the book of Ephesians chapter 6. It tells you to first put on the breastplate of righteousness, which means to align your heart with the will of God. Simply put, don't forget your raincoat. Being emotionally intelligent is a major article of clothing in your spiritual wardrobe.

Have you ever wondered what was it that caused Moses to fall short, and not enter into the promise land? Well, the answer was his anger, or his emotions. What causes someone to commit a murder in a fit of passion? It's their emotions. If your emotions are not lined up with the will of God they will cause you to act irrationally, and many times out of character. When you are acting out of pure emotions, it hinders your ability to think logically. It clouds your vision, and it closes the door to better judgment. You must learn to control your emotions, and not allow your emotions to control you. That is why the Lord tells us in the book of Proverbs 2:10 & 11:

When wisdom entereth into thine heart, and knowledge is pleasant unto thy soul; Discretion shall preserve thee, and understanding shall keep thee;

When your emotions are in line you are not so quick to act, but you will evaluate your situation for what it is. Then move accordingly to the inclinations and the resolutions of God.

Ephesians also tells us to have our feet shod or covered with the gospel of peace, which acts as our rain boots. In other words we are to have our feet firmly planted on the word of God, and standing on His promises. In the midst of a storm it is easy to slip. At times we will get tired of fighting the rain, and that is when we will begin to look for the quickest way out. Many of us have given up on life, and we have begun to accept things just as they are. We have looked at the world around us, and we've picked up the spirit of, if you can't beat them then you might as well join them.

There are mighty men of God working long hours, trying to do what's right, trying to provide for their families, and instead of getting ahead they're falling behind at break neck speed. Then they begin to look at the guys standing on the street corners, the guys in the music videos, the one's that are driving the fast cars, spending lots of money, and are surrounded by beautiful women, and that is when their feet begin to slip.

Then there are the beautiful women of God, who are raising a family, working, running a household, and playing the role of mother, counselor, and wife. That are much too often over looked, over worked, and under appreciated. Their husbands never pay them any attention, their bosses never give them the respect that they deserve, and their children never give them any rest. Then they begin to get frustrated, and their feet begin to slip. They begin to feel like Asaph, when he said in the book of Psalms 73:2:

But as for me, my feet were almost gone; my steps had well nigh slipped.

In the midst of a storm it is easy to give up, and your feet can and will slip if they are not firmly planted on a solid foundation. That is why you must stand with the assurance that God will provide, and no matter what situation that you may find yourself in you have got to know without a shadow of a doubt that the Lord will see you through.

Ephesians goes on to tell us to take the shield of faith so that we will be able to quench all the fiery darts of the wicked, or it tells us to bring an umbrella. The shield of faith is meant to block or deflect the attacks of the enemy. If we were to think back to the African tribesmen going off to battle we would find a very important concept. One of the main pieces of their battle gear would be their shield. These great warriors would carry these very large shields in front of them that would rise above their heads, and go down until they would actually touch the ground. These shields were designed to protect the warrior completely. Much like the shield of faith was created to protect the saints of God.

Coming Out of the Rain

We are to carry our faith with us in such a way that it encompasses us completely. Knowing that whatever comes our way, we are covered. Knowing that no matter what attack the enemy tries against us we are covered. If he tries to attack the head, we're covered. If he tries to attack the chest, were covered. If he tries to attack the feet, we are still covered. We are covered because the Bible promise in the book of Isaiah 54:17:

No weapon that is formed against thee shall prosper; and every tongue that shall rise against thee in judgment thou shalt condemn. This is the heritage of the servants of the Lord, and their righteousness is of me, saith the Lord.

Pastor Charles C. Brown

Your faith is meant to cover you, like an umbrella is meant to protect you from a downpour. As long as you stay under the umbrella you will remain dry, and as long as you stay under your shield of faith you will remain covered.

Ephesians tells us to take the helmet of salvation, which is considered to be our rain hats. The helmet of salvation is meant to protect your mind. The enemy knows that if he can get you to think that you are defeated then you will be defeated. If he can plant a seed of doubt, despair, hopelessness, or confusion than the battle will be over before it ever gets started. The word of God states in Proverbs 23:6:

For as he (man) thinketh in his heart, so is he:

If the enemy can make you think that you are sick, then you will be sick. If the enemy can get you to think that you are dying then you will die. If the enemy can get you to think that you will never make it, then you won't. You have to make it a habit of thinking positive thoughts, believing positive ideas, and speaking positive words.

For death and life are in the power of the tongue.

(Proverbs 18:21)

You have to guard your thoughts against even the smallest seed of negativity. Because if you don't than the smallest seed will take root, and grow into a massive Redwood of negative thoughts and energy. Smothering every flower of imagination, and blocking every ray of hope for a brighter tomorrow. The helmet of salvation is meant to protect you from that, and to align your thoughts with the will of God. For the Bible says in Isaiah 26:3:

Thou wilt keep him in perfect peace, whose mind is stayed on thee.

When you are dressed for the weather, the winds may blow, and the storms may rage, but you are covered. You are covered from the crown of your head to the soles of your feet. When you are dealing with a storm you must be prepared for anything that may come your way. You must be prepared for who ever, and whatever the enemy has in store for you, for where there is no preparation there will be no graduation.

Chapter 4

No Signs Of Letting Up.

The funny thing about a storm is at times it can seem as though the rain will never end. Have you ever had one of those days when it seemed as though it would rain forever? You had made the perfect plans, the perfect preparations, and the perfect provisions. Everything was packed, and ready to go. You were prepared for everything except the weather. It was your big day. The day that for as long as you could remember you had been waiting for, longing for, and hoping for, and now it was finally here. You had chosen to be wed in an elegant outdoor setting. The flowers were beautifully arrayed, the seats were arranged perfectly, and there you were the beautiful bride making your way down the aisle in a stunning one of a kind wedding dress. Then without notice the clouds burst open, and brought forth a sea of rain.

Now if we were to bring it even closer to home, it always seems as though when one thing goes wrong everything else is bound to go wrong. Our problems tend to start out as small as a snowflake, but over the course of time they tend to grow into monstrous proportion covering our lives like an avalanche one thing leading to another. One problem adding up to another, and it keeps going and growing until you are buried under the pressure.

There is an old cliché that says, "When it rains it pours," and does that not sound like many of our situations? The telephone bill is due, the gas just been disconnected, the rent is two months behind, you just lost your dog, your supposedly better half has left you for someone younger, your job has just announce that your whole department is being down sized, and you are next in line to be let go. Now here you are caught in the middle of a downpour, and it's not showing any signs of letting up.

As I look back over my life, I often wonder how did I make it through? It seems as though my personal storm lasted for years. There was a time in my life when I wore the cloud of despair, like a tailor made suit. It fit me perfectly, and no matter how hard I tried I could not take it off. I was stuck. I had my own personal rain cloud that followed me everywhere that I went. It rained in my personal life. It rained in my professional life. It rained in my spiritual life, and it even showed signs of raining in my future life. I was water logged down to the very depths of my soul, and we must remember that water weighs you down.

Water adds pounds to your load, and puts extra ballast on your ship. The more problems you have the heavier your load becomes. No matter how light your outerwear may be, if you get caught out in the rain you will feel the weight. The weight of your clothes is multiplied by the taking on of water, and the longer you stay out in the rain the heavier your clothing becomes. And the heavier your clothing becomes, the harder it is to carry that load around. So what do you do?

Many of us are fighting with that same question. We are wondering what am I going to do? If I keep going ahead I may get lost in the storm, and if I turn around and go back I may miss my blessing. In the midst of a downpour it is easy to become disoriented. It's easy to lose your heading, and miss judge your bearing.

Coming Out of the Rain

While driving down the highway of life in a storm, at times it can rain so hard that you cannot see the taillights of the car that is directly in front of you. Your windshield wipers are working as fast as they can, but they just can't seem to move the water quick enough. If you are not careful you may very well end up on the side of the road in a ditch, with no help in sight for miles around. So when the rain seems like it is not going to end, always remember this one thing. Stay clam! Never let the devil see you sweat.

If you keep your head, you can make it through the storm. This is not the time to give up. This is the time to pray. Now is the time to exercise those prayer muscles. You have got to pray until you get an answer, or a sign that the rain is going to stop. You must take on the spirit of David when he said:

As for me, I will call upon God; and the Lord shall save me. Evening, and morning, and at noon, will I pray, and cry aloud: and he shall hear my voice. (Psalm 55:16-17)

When you can't see your way through, you've got to pray your way through. Prayer is the key that unlocks the door to your break through. Through prayer your request is made known unto God. That is why the word of God says in Luke 18&1 that:

Man ought always to pray, and not to faint.

Because when your prayer life is in order you can take your petitions to the Lord, with the assurances that he will answer your prayers. When your prayer life is in order, if the Lord our God does not stop the rain, he will give you the patience that it takes to wait out the storm. In your time of storm you not only have to pray for, but you also must know how to pray.

There are different types of prayers, but we will be dealing with three distinct types: Petitions, Intercessions, and prayers of Communion. Each prayer has a distinct purpose, and if your prayers are going to have power than you must know which type of prayer to use.

In prayers of Petitions you are asking the Lord to do something for you. You are giving the Lord a formal request to do something on your behalf. You are telling the Lord that you need help. You are not praying for you mother, your father, your children, or your friends. You are praying that the Lord would move your mountain, or give you the strength to withstand the storm. In the book of Judges 16:29 Samson made his request known unto God for he said:

O Lord, remember me, I pray thee, and strengthen me.

Samson was in the midst of his storm, and it seemed as though the rain would never end. He was in need of a deliverance, and a break through. So he had to look past his resources, and go straight to the source. He looked up to Heaven, and said, "Lord Help!" That is why a constant prayer life is a must. You cannot wait until you are in the midst of the storm, and then start praying. Your prayer life must be in order before you get to the storm. In order to have an effective prayer life you must first have a relationship with the Lord. Don't wait until the last minute to try and establish a relationship with God. Put the time in early, and then have some timber stored up in Heaven. That is what Paul meant in 1 Timothy 6:19 when he said;

Laying up in store for themselves a good foundation against the time come.

So that when the time comes to call on the Lord, you have some prayers stored in His spiritual bank. You cannot make a withdrawal unless you have made a deposit, or your receipt will come back with the message "insufficient funds" account closed!

The second type of prayers is prayer of Intercession. Here you are praying the God would do something through you. In these prayers you are actually intervening, or standing in the gap for someone else. You are standing in proxy for a loved one, friend, fellow saint, or sinner and this is where prayer partners are the most important.

At times when you are in the midst of the storm, you need the prayers of the saints to help pull you through. You have to start surrounding yourself with prayer warriors that you know can get a prayer through. You must have praying saints in your life that you can call on and say, "Lets pray." And not have to worry about telling them everything that's going on in your life, their just ready to pray. You don't have to tell them all the details. You don't have to give them all the ins and outs. They are not trying to pry into your affairs. They're not trying to get into your business. They're just ready to pray until your situation starts to change. That is why James the brother of Jesus said that:

Pastor Charles C. Brown

The effectual fervent prayer of a righteous man availeth much. (James 5:16)

Because when true saints start praying, things begin to happen. Situations start to turn around. Bodies are healed, minds are restored, marriages are fixed, children are delivered, and storms are subdued. You must surround yourself with praying people, for there is power in prayer.

The third type of prayer is a prayer of Communion. Here you are asking the Lord to do something within you. When the storm is raging, and the wind is blowing it is easy to become upset, confused, frustrated, tired, afraid, bewildered, or doubtful. It happened to Peter, when he walked on the water to meet Jesus. The word of God say's in the book of Matthew 14:30:

When he saw the wind boisterous, he was afraid;

When the rain will not stop falling, and the wind will not stop blowing it is a perfect opportunity for the enemy to come in and whisper a word of doubt in your ear. It is easy to look around at your situation, and begin to get afraid of failing. When fear sets up shop, it becomes very easy to lose faith.

So instead of giving in to despair, turn it over to prayer, and begin to Commune with the Lord. Open your heart unto Him, and ask Him to come in. In this sacred time of prayer make your heart available to the will of God. Ask the Lord to come into your soul, and ease your troubled mind. Ask the Lord to come into your heart, and remove all doubt. Ask the Lord to come into your spirit, and take away your fears. You must stand before the Lord, like an empty pitcher begging the Lord to fill you up. You must acquire the spirit of David, when he said in the book of Psalms 51:10:

Create in me a clean heart, O God, and renew a right spirit in me.

When it looks as though the rain will never cease form falling, instead of looking around at your situation look to the Lord for your direction.

Chapter 5

Standing Alone In The Strom.

One of the worst feelings that you can have is that you are all alone, and that feeling is multiplied greatly in your time of storm. At times in our hour of crisis we feel that no one understands us, no one can or is willing to help, and no one knows what we're going through. It seems as though everyone that we turn to just cannot comprehend the full ramifications of our circumstances.

It seems that no one understands that by nature man is drawn to man, and that we get a feeling of completeness from one another, and when we are in the midst of a storm that is when we need that feeling of completeness the most. That is when we need that feeling of belonging that we can only acquire from another person the most. It is almost detrimental to our spirit, when we cannot find that wholeness in the ones that we call dear.

Loneliness can be a killer in its self. One of the biggest causes of suicide is the feeling that you are in this world all alone. When you look around and see people laughing, loving, and living life to the fullest with other people the pain can become excruciating. If we are not careful at this time the loneliness can bring on the spirit of sadness, sadness can bring on the spirit of depression, depression can bring on the spirit of desperation, and desperation can bring on the spirit of hopelessness. And where there is no hope, there are no dreams for the future.

Now I am not talking about those individuals who are introverted, or who enjoy being by themselves. I am talking about those who are extroverted, or those who enjoy, and at times even thrive off the company of others. We may not understand it, but many times we get our strength from those who are around us. And when we cannot get that extra push that we need, many times we tend to stop fighting. We just give up, and accept our fate.

That is why in our times of loss, when we are getting over addictions, in times of divorce, and in countless other situations many people recommend that we seek the help of some type of support group. Because in those low periods we need to hear other people say, "I have been there, I made it out, and so can you." But when we cannot find that group, or when we just can't seem to somehow fit in, giving up seems to be our only alternative. David himself said in the book of Psalm 55:6:

Oh that I had wings like a dove! For then would I fly away, and be at rest.

At that moment in time, when you've tried everything and nothing seems to be going right. The only thing that you want to do is get away. The only thing that you want to find is some level of peace. The only thing that your heart truly desires is to find rest for your weary soul. And it can be very confusing, because many times there is a battle raging on the inside of you. A battle that's tearing you apart, where you are torn between standing to fight, or putting as much distance between you and your problems that is humanly possible. There is an uncontrolled battle raging on the inside of you, and if you are not careful it can drive you mad. To quote an old cliché, "It's like being caught between a rock and a hard place."

Pastor Charles C. Brown

There was a time in my life, when the only thing that I wanted to do was run away. Everything that I started had failed, and everything that I touched was destroyed. At that time when I needed my so-called friends the most, they were nowhere to be found. All I had left were those bitter sweet tears that seemed to burst from my eyes, as though the dam that held them back for so long had been somehow blown away by the forces of nature.

At that moment when I was all alone, it seemed like there was no way out. All kinds of thoughts ran through my mind. I began to contemplate things that were far beyond my normal imagination. Those were some of the darkest days of my life. At that point I felt like a rowboat in the middle of the Atlantic Ocean, and I was beginning to sink for I had begun to take on water. My storm had just begun, and along with it came 20 feet waves. The sharks were circling, and there was not another boat in sight. At that moment I felt as though all hope was gone, and my life was about to end. I was anchorless.

But at the crucial moment instead of giving up, and admitting defeat I decided to search deep within my soul, and that is where I found the Lord. Instead of looking around for help from an outside force I had to depend upon the force that had been there all along. I had finally realized that the only way out of my storm was with the help of God. I was never truly aware of it, but all throughout my ordeal the Lord was trying to get my attention. Because out of all the scriptures that I knew by heart the only one that played continuously in my mind was Matthew 11:28 where Jesus said:

Come unto me, all ye that labor and are heavy laden, and I will give you rest.

All the struggling that I was doing was brought on by my own failure to hear what the Lord was saying to me. All the while he was saying, "My child I'm right here, and all you have to do is reach out to me." But instead of turning to Him, I turned to man. That is when I found out; when you need man the most he will let you down every time. And it took my so-called friends to actually walk away from me, before I began to realize that I must depend on the Lord and no one else. I learned that the more that I depended on the Lord the easier it became to endure the storm.

The funny thing about all of this was, while I was walking alone in the storm, things were beginning to change around me and within me. I was use to people pleasing. I wanted to be liked by people so much that many times I would go above, and beyond that which was asked of me just so that my friends would accept me. I would bend over backwards, and even go out of my way to please others. But while I was trying to please others, I was losing who I was. I was wearing so many masks that it came a time in my life, when I had to tell myself would the real Charles C. Brown please stand up.

Although I wanted to stop, I was so use to people pleasing that it had become second nature. And no longer was I surrounded by the people that I once knew and loved, but now I was surrounded by a bunch of strangers that could care less about my well being. I felt like a clown in the circus jumping through hoops trying to please my audience. But while I was in the storm, those very same individuals were being washed away. The more it rained the less they would come around, and the closer I got to God. In the midst of the storm I was being pruned. The Lord was cutting away my dead branches, and replacing them with fresh vibrant ones, for He said in John 15:2:

Every branch in me that bearth not fruit he taketh away: and every branch that bearth fruit, he purgeth it, that it may bring forth more fruit.

I was growing, but I was not growing properly. My branches were growing wildly, and in all of the wrong directions. So in the midst of the storm the master gardener was replanting me, and making me better. If I said that, "This was a painless situation." I would be lying because it was painful. It hurt a great deal. I was use to having a large group of people around me at all times. I was use to being in the midst of a crowd, and to have all of that taken away form me suddenly was like having my whole world turned upside down.

When a tree is being pruned, the dead branches are cut away. And at times you may even have to cut away some healthy branches, in order to make room for even healthier ones. While going through this process I could not understand everything that was going on around me. I knew why my so called friends have had to leave, but what about the ones that were really my friends, who had been there for me from the very first day? I did not understand it then, but I can understand it now. The Lord wanted me to depend completely and totally on Him. Because in the midst of it all, I began to look past what man thought of me, and began to totally concentrate on what the Lord was thinking of me. Instead of trying to please man, I began to try to please God.

In the rain when my clown face was washed away the real me began to emerge. I began to realize that if someone was only my friend because of what I could do for them, or for what I had then that same someone was never really a true friend from the beginning. If your friends were only around you in the good times, but in the bad times they turned and walked away then they were never your friends.

Ironically, the more I was alone, the more I became aware of who I truly was. No longer was I trying to please people with what I had, or with what I could do, but now I was allowing them to accept me for I was.

I became a loner in the storm, and that is when the storm began to become my instructor. It began to teach me self-confidence, acceptance, and assurance that my life, my dreams, and my feelings did matter. It taught me not only to accept me for me, but it also taught me how to love me. I began to realize that everyone is not going to like me, and at times I may have to walk alone, but my world will not end because life does go on.

Chapter 6

A Leaky Roof.

Your house is meant to be your shelter in the time of storm. When the wind is blowing fiercely, and the snow is falling brutally your shelter is your protector. When the temperature is severely dropping, and the raindrops are pounding against your windowsill your warm and cozy castle was designed to keep you safe and sound. However, there are instances when your utopia can become disrupted, and much too often it's at the most inconvenient time.

Pastor Charles C. Brown

It seems as though the furnace always goes out on the coldest winter night, and that is the hardest concept to comprehend. It is easy to deal with a problem when you are expecting it, but what about when you thought that you were prepared? Or better yet what about when you were expecting something, or someone to keep you safe from all harm, and then they let you down? Is that not a fate that many would deem worst than death?

When we are relying totally on something, or someone it can give us a false since of hope. We tend to tell ourselves that at least I've got this to fall back on, or at least I have that to pull me through, and that is when we begin to lose our focus. Because we begin to believe that our shelters are our safe havens, and the powers of darkness and all of their forces can only get as close as the front door. No matter how bad our day may have gone, if can just turn onto our blocks, and can just barely see our homes we begin to feel just a little bit better. When we pull into our driveways, or park in front of our homes, when we stick our keys into the door, turn the knob, walk inside, and kick off our shoes we instantly get a feeling of relief.

We often feel that we may have to take orders at work, and we may have to look over our shoulders outside, but once we enter into our sanctuaries we can declare asylum. In our shelters we are free. Free to be our selves. We don't have to pretend to be someone, or something that we are not. In our sanctuaries we are free to bask in the glory of seclusion. Now at times this strong sense of security can set us up for a big fall because believe it or not it can be a false sense of safety. For the very same thing that we put our trust in can be the very same thing that let us down in the long run, and at times this can be very difficult to deal with, and that is why we must learn how to put our trust in the one sure thing that will never fail. We must learn how to trust in the Lord. We must learn how to totally depend on the Lord, for He is the one sure thing that will never let us down.

Coming Out of the Rain

I am not suggesting that you become cold, and withdrawn from the world that is surrounding you. I am only suggesting that you keep your vision in the right focus. You must learn how to stop looking to, and depending on the things in which you are able to see with your natural eye. And begin to rely on the one thing that you cannot see, but you know with all of your heart is there. You must learn how to lean on the Lord. That is what the Apostle Paul meant when he said:

While we look not at the things which are seen, but at the things which are not seen: for the things which are seen are temporal; but the things which are not seen are eternal. (2 Corinthians 4:18)

In all of its excellence, and in all of it's beauty our shelters are still only brick and mortar. It still has flaws and cracks under the surface that we may not be able to see. And if we approach life with this open frame of mind, it better prepares us for life's unexpected circumstances. Many of us are walking through life with blinders on, and when problems come they tend to cause more damage than they should.

There are certain precautions that we are able to utilize that will better prepare us for a storm. And these precautions are simply trusting in the Lord at all times, adhering to the warning signs, which are our indicators that trouble may very well be on the way, and most of all we must be prepared to do something about our situations. Before your roof started leaking there were signs of damage, but many times we allowed those signs to go unnoticed. The first time that you noticed watermarks on the ceiling should have been your sign that there may be trouble. When you saw the plaster was beginning to fall around your head, that was a sign that something was going wrong, and that repairs may be in order. And when you allowed those signs to go unnoticed, you were allowing the problems to get bigger, and cause more damage.

For instance one of the most sacred institutions in life is marriage, and many of us have found a shelter from the storm within them. And that is the way that God meant it to be, but even in our marriages we must still trust in the Lord, and watch out for those leaks. If in our unions we were to begin to utilize these two beneficial concepts divorce courts would cease to exist, and families would stay together.

We must begin to realize that the foundations of our marriages are actually made up of multiple concepts that must be cultivated, and nourished through out our unions. These concepts are love, trust, communication, understanding, and undying commitment. If we were to allow these concepts to wither away so will our marriages. When these concepts are somehow overlooked, or underestimated our roofs begin to leak. And before long what was once a beautiful home filled with many hopes and dreams, has been transformed into a dwindling shack on the verge of being condemned. Now you must begin to realize that it did not get this way overnight the signs were there, but you chose to ignore them.

Within the marriage when the roof began to leak, many of us chose to look the other way. We swept the problems under the rug. We did not want to make any waves, nor did we want to cause any problems. And in the midst of not wanting to cause any problems, the lines of communications began to break down. Now what had started out as small as a simple leak has been transformed into a major downpour.

When we met that special person for the first time, we would talk for hours at a time about anything and everything under the sun. But soon after we said, "I do," those very same conversations that would go on for hours were exchanged for slamming doors, dirty looks, and late nights at the office. And believe it or not the roof was leaking, and it could have been repaired.

We must always remember that our foundational concepts are love, trust, communication, and commitment. And when the roof begins to leak, these are the tools that are within our spiritual toolboxes, or that are on our spiritual tool belts that we must utilize in order to make those necessary repairs. In our time of despair instead of giving up, and admitting defeat we must reach for our tools and begin to reconstruct! After we have gathered the right tools, and put on our work clothes it is now time to reach for the manual, which in fact is the word of God. When we are completely and totally prepared for the job that is at hand, we can finally get to work.

When the repairs are underway, we must always remember the love that we share with that special person. People often say that, "Love conquers all," and that is especially true when dealing with the concept of marriage. If we can remember that this is the person that we vowed to love for richer or for poorer, in sickness and in health until death do us part, if we can remember our vows, and the reasons behind our vows then we will have something to hold onto. Then no matter what comes our way we can rest assure that together we can conquer all, and through the love that we share nothing will be impossible. That is why Paul said in Ephesians 5:25:

Husbands, love your wives, even as Christ also loved the church, and gave himself for it;

In dealing with the concept of love we must realize that it is not what we can get, but it's what we can give. Many times we have to give all that we have in the name of love in order for our love to last. When we are willing to sacrifice in the name of love, we are willing to see our marriage last forever. Realizing that the greatest sacrifice that we can offer is a sacrifice of self. Jesus himself gave his life for a sinner like me, and in doing so He made the ultimate sacrifice. If Jesus loves me that much, shouldn't I also be willing to make a sacrifice for the ones that I claim to love?

After love comes trust, which is one of the hardest tools to master, especially if we have been emotionally scared in the past, but nevertheless in spite of the pain we must learn how to trust, which in many cases can be a very long, slow, and demandingly grueling process. Trusting in someone else means that we are not going to question him or her every time they leave. Trusting in someone means that we are not going to follow him or her around everywhere they go. We have to realize that the concept behind trusting is simply letting go, and letting God.

We have to understand that trust is something that is built over time, and with trust comes responsibility. Because that same trust that was built over many years can be destroyed in a matter of seconds, and once that trust is destroyed it can take years to rebuild, if it is ever to be rebuilt. Lying, being deceitful, using deception, and delusions are all tools used to undermine the very same thing that you are trying to build. In a marriage we must be open and honest to the fullest extent. When we are being dishonest to our spouses in actuality we are being dishonest to ourselves, for when we are in a marriage are we two not one? The Lord said in the book of Genesis 2:24:

Therefore shall a man leave his father and his mother, and shall cleave unto his wife: and they shall be one flesh.

That is why the concept of trust is so important because the individuals that we are married to become a major part of our lives. In dealing with the concept of marriage we must learn to trust in the

Lord more so than ever before. We must know without a shadow of a doubt that this is the individual that the Lord our God intended for us to spend the rest of our lives with. When we know this deep within our spirits, when the problems arrive we can boldly go before the throne of grace, and tell the Lord that, "You gave me my spouse, and now Lord you must fix my situation." Then we can step back, and let God handle it. We must trust in the Lord whole heartily, and believe that He will see us through.

Along with love and trust comes commitment, which far too often is taken entirely to lightly. We fail to realize that a relationship of any type must have a level of commitment on all sides in order for it to work. We must be committed to making the necessary sacrifices, and adjustments that it takes to make our unions the best that they could possibly be. Commitment means that we are not going to take off running at the first sign of trouble. Commitment means that we are not going to enter into our relationships, with the stipulations, that if things do not go exactly as we planned then there is always divorce court, as if marriages came with a revolving door. Commitment means that we are there for the long haul, or as our vows stated, "Until death do us part." Commitment means divorce is not even an option, for Jesus said in the book of Matthew 5:32:

Whosoever shall put away his wife, saving for the cause of fornication, causeth her to commit adultery: and whosoever shall marry her that is divorced committeth adultery.

Commitment means that there is a continuing obligation, or a promise on your part that you will do whatever it takes in order to make our marriages the best that they can be. A committed saint can fix a leaking roof, and repair a shattered home.

Now in order to be fully committed you must first have an understanding of what, or whom we are committed to. And in order to understand someone we must first open our hearts to the Lord, so that it may be renewed. That is what David meant when he said:

Create in me a clean heart, O God; and renew a right spirit within me.

An understanding heart is able to give wholly of oneself, without expecting anything in return. Being able to give of oneself allows us to tare down the walls that we have erected through out the years, and it also allows us to become closer to the ones that we love. To truly understand someone means that we would never do anything to him or her that we would not want him or her to do unto us. An understanding heart is one that is filled with compassion and emotions. For compassion in a heart is like a sealer to a leak, it strengthens the bond.

Which brings us back to communication all of these concepts are hinged upon the channels of communication. The only way that we can have a strong, and healthy relationship is through an open channel of communication. We cannot have trust, commitment, understanding, or love without having a strong line of communication. If we could trace the leak back to its origins we would find that it started out as a break down within the lines of communication. We stopped growing, when we stopped talking.

Communication allows us to let our feelings be known. Many people believe that by their actions, or body language others should know how they feel. Now that is true to a certain extent. But when we open our mouths we remove all doubt, and allow people to know exactly what is on our minds. It also allows our petitions to be known unto the Lord our God. It gives us the opportunity to speak a blessing into our relationships. If we want our relationships to be prosperous we must speak prosperity into existence. We must learn how to use the power of our words. The Apostle John made an astonishing revelation when he said,

In the beginning was the Word, and the word was with God, and the Word was God. The same was in the beginning with God. All things were made by him, and without him was not any thing that was made. (John 1:1-3)

If we want life in our relationships we must speak life into existence. Not only should we speak it, we must also believe that it will come to past. We must realize that everything is hinged upon the word.

Far too often when our roofs are leaking we tend to either climb up and apply a patch to them, or add some extra tar, which in fact is only a temporary fix. Many of us have patched up, and bandaged up our relationships for so long that we are beginning to look like mummies. We have failed to realize that much to often when a roof is leaking the water may be dripping in the back of the house, but the actual hole may very well be in the front of the house. What we may not be able to see or understand is how water can travel through many unseen crevices and channels until it finds a proper outlet. So instead of patching up the old roof, we must develop a plan that will enable us to completely remove it, and replace it with a new one. And if we were to take out a moment to be truthful with ourselves, we would find that the majority of us are in desperate need of a complete replacement.

Pastor Charles C. Brown

Some of us need to take out a little time and completely overhaul our relationships. We need to get rid of all of the hurt, and the pain and start our livers over again. We need to start over on a clean slate, leveling off all of the bumps and lumps, and filling in all of the cracks that were caused by all of the hurt and the pain in the beginning. We need to rebuild the trust, nourish the love, strengthen the commitment, open our hearts to understanding those that are in our lives, and open the channels of communication with the ones we love. When your roof is leaking don't move out, just grab your tools and go to work. And not only will your home look better, but your property value will increase.

Chapter 7

Taking Charge of the Storm.

In order to overcome your storm there is a certain level of spirituality that you must strive to achieve. You must get to a level in life, where you begin to say, "Enough is enough." Where you begin to call off that pity party, get off that soapbox, and hang up your suit of sorrow. You must make it to the level, where you are ready to fight with every ounce of strength that you have left. Where in your ring of life, when you hear the bell ring you go to your corner, and come out fighting. When you are tired of feeling sorry for yourself, and tired of settling for less than you are worth, when you are tired of just excepting anything that the devil has to throw at you, and now you are ready to start throwing back. When you reach that level in life, you are ready to take charge of your storm.

When you begin to realize that a storm only has three levels, the manner in which you perceive your situations begin to redefine its self. You begin to look at your circumstances from a different point of view, and from an entirely different prospective. Your entire frame of mind begins to change, and the manner in which you think begins to redevelop its self on a higher spiritual plane. In chapter three we briefly touched upon the importance of protecting your mind from the influences of the enemy. When you are dealing with the three stages of a storm not only must you protect your mind, but you must also renew your mind, for if we are not careful instead of overcoming the storm, we will become a part of the storm. That is why the Apostle Paul said in Romans 12&2:

Be not conformed to this world: but be ye transformed by the renewing of your mind.

Renewing your mind allows you to see the storm for what it is, and not only see the storm, but it also gives you the strength to rise above it. It helps you to realize that a storm can only be either in the beginning stage, which is when the drizzling starts.

In the middle stage, which is the downpour, or the final stage, which is the breaking point. Renewing your mind helps you to determine what must be done in order to survive your ordeal. Determining the level of the storm allows you to pace yourself, store up some prayers, and prepare yourself for the long haul. Determining your level of the storm allows you the opportunity to refocus your vision, and readjust your sights.

Each one of these three levels has a distinct characteristic, and a distinct set of qualities and attributes. These idiosyncrasies will give you the insight that it takes to easily distinguish these levels from one another. When it begins to drizzle, which in actuality is the beginning stage. That is the sign that a storm is on the way. When the dark clouds begin to roll in, and the sky begins to darken these are warning signs. When the wind begins to pick up, and you can smell the rain in the air these are the signs that you should begin to prepare yourself for a storm. Many people will even go as far as to say that, "When a storm is coming you can feel it in your bones."

If you were to take heed to all of these signs you would be able to prepare yourself for whatever was coming your way. Realizing that change is in the air should be a warning sign to proceed with caution, and to make you aware that a detour may be up ahead. When it starts drizzling many of us tend to look at it as being no big deal, and instead of running for shelter or getting out their umbrellas they continue to go about their business as though nothing is going on, and when the clouds burst they're caught off guard. The beginning stage is so important because it sets the precedence for what is to come.

Now I am not suggesting that you walk around on pins and needles watching and waiting for something to go wrong. I am merely suggesting that you become more aware of your surroundings, and begin to pay special attention to the warning signs. When your job began cutting back that was a warning signs. When your significant other spent more time away from you than with you, that was a warning signs. When you had to have a drink before you went to sleep, and one when you woke up that was a warning signs. When they began downsizing the department down the hall from yours, that was a warning sign and a half that something was about to happen. When you saw that first sign, you should have been preparing yourself to take precautionary measures.

And as I said earlier, "Where many of us go wrong is that we allow these signs to go unnoticed," and what started out as small as a snow flake has grown into an avalanche burying everything in its path. When we allow our problems to get to a level that we feel is too big for us to handle, we have a tendency of giving up, and for many of us giving up is the easiest thing to do. When you feel as though no matter what you do, it's not going to work you tend to give up. When you have tried and tried, and things seem as though they are getting worst instead of better, sooner or later you are going to stop trying, and that is exactly what the devil wants you to do.

The devil knows that if he can get you to give up in the beginning, then the victory shall be his. If he can get you to admit defeat at the onset of the storm, then he knows that there is no way in the world that you are going to make it to the end, but what you must realize is that Solomon said in Ecclesiastes 9:11:

The race is not giving to the swift, nor the battle to the strong.

You have got to endure the race until the end. You must begin to say to yourself, "Come hell, or high water I am going to make it through." You have got to put it in your spirit that giving up is not even an option. That giving up is not one of your choices. Others may give up, but you will run on until the end. You may not come in first, or second but you will finish the race. In the beginning, when it starts to drizzle that is the time to make up in you mind that no matter what may come your way, you will not quit.

When you have that frame of mind, and when your conviction is that strong God begins to work on your behalf. When you can tell the devil, "I won't quit," God tells you that, "I am with you, and I will see you through." When your mind is made up, your body can't help but to follow. When you are surrounded by positive energy, there is no room for negative forces. When the light is shining within you, God is working through you, and the devil has no power over you. When you stand up to weather the storm, you are not standing alone. You are standing with the Almighty God, who can and will make a way out of no way. In the very beginning you must set your mind on going through, and not giving up. Then no mater what happens, you can stand tall like the Apostle Paul who said in 2 Timothy 4:7:

I have fought a good fight, I have finished my course, I have kept the faith:

Then you can stand tall under the anointing of God, and proclaim with a loud voice that, "The storm could not beat me because I beat it." In the beginning you must make the claim that you will come out the victor, and not the victim. Grab the storm by the horns, and command it to submit unto the power of God. You must refuse to settle for nothing less than total submission. From the first sign of rain prepare yourself to take charge of your storm.

The middle stage, or the downpour is one of the hardest stages to understand. Because here is where the majority of us will decide to give up, and throw in the towel. At this level the rain is falling so fiercely, and the winds are blowing so harshly that it can become blinding. At times the storm can become so fierce that we may become disoriented and confused. We can become so confused that we don't know which way to turn, or which way to go, so many times we end up just giving up. This is a dangerous place to be in because here is where you either make it, or break it. Here is where you either conquer the storm, or the storm will conquer you. The reason why this stage of the storm is so fierce is because here is where you will get the most out of your ordeal.

In the downpour you character is shaped, your faith is strengthened, and your relationship with God is fortified. Your character determines how you will handle trials, tribulations, and circumstances that will arise in your everyday life. If you never decide to stand up for what you believe in, and face your storm you will become someone who avoids confrontations at all cost. Instead of living your life to the fullest, you will spend it running and in constant fear of the world that you are living in. On the other hand, if you spend your life rushing into everything you will become someone who never takes the time to truly sit back, and evaluate your situations. Then you will spend the rest of your days rushing into battles that should have been avoided.

So in the downpour the Lord begins to fashion a storm that will instill within you the right amount of patience, and the right amount of ambition that it takes for you to handle life's problem in a godly manner. That is why the Lord said in the book of Isaiah 43:2:

When thou passest through the waters, I will be with thee; and through the rivers, they shall not

overflow thee; when thou walkest through the fire, thou shalt not be burned; neither shall the flame kindle upon thee.

For the Lord our God has shaped the storm to fit you, and he has formed you to withstand the storm. If God never makes you go through anything than how will you know how strong you truly are? You must realize that in this life your character can take you further than your gifts, or your talents will ever be able to. The Lord wants you to be able to go into any setting and into any situation, and still maintain a godly demeanor. So in the storm your mannerisms are developed, and you also begin to do more listening and less talking. You begin to develop a heart of love, and a mind of understanding. You begin to develop warmth and compassion for your brother man, you begin to feel, and most importantly you begin to live again.

In the downpour the Lord will put you into a situation, where you must depend totally on Him and only Him, and this will cause your faith to become strengthened. As long as you know where your next meal is coming from there is no need to seek the Lord, but when you don't know what to do, and where to go that is when you're forced to depend on the Lord. The Lord knows that the entire concept of your religion is based upon your faith. He knows that the level of your faith measures the level of your power, and in order to have much power you must have much faith. The best definition of faith is found in Hebrews 11:1 where the Apostle Paul said:

Now faith is the substance of things hoped for, the evidence of things not seen.

In the midst of the storm you must know without a shadow of a doubt that the Lord will supply your every need, and that He will see you through. Your faith must be unwavering, and although you may not be able to see how you're gong to make it you must know that you will. It takes faith to please God, and when all else fails your faith is the only thing that you will be able to rely upon. Your faith is your undying commitment and belief in God without question. And in the downpour, when you begin to realize that it was nothing but a God that could have sustained you in your time of need your faith is stamped with the seal of approval by the Almighty God himself.

Now in order for you to have faith in something or someone you must first have a relationship with them. You must understand that the best definition of a relationship is the terms in which one person has dealings with another. And the term that forms the bases of your relationship with God in its simplest form is that, if you serve Him, He will take care of you. For the Apostle Paul said in the book of Philippians 4&19:

My God shall supply all your need according to his riches in glory by Christ Jesus.

Your relationship with God is sealed with a promise, commitment, or covenant. And in the midst of the storm as you begin to grow closer and closer to Him, your covenant or promise becomes stronger and stronger. Than you begin to realize that the further you go the more you begin to grow. For the Lord our God has given you His promise that He would take care of you, but you must first begin to depend on Him. In actuality your relationship with God flows in two distinct directions. God has promised you in His word that He would take care of you if you would follow Him. On the other hand, you promised the Lord that you would follow Him if he took care of you. So in the midst of walking through the storm, as you are trusting in Him, He is making a way for you. And as He is making a way for you, you are trusting in Him. Until you become totally depended upon Him, and He is totally committed to taking care of you, and you and the Lord become as one. When the rain is falling around you, God becomes your umbrella, and your shelter in the time of storm.

When I found myself in the midst of a downpour, I though that I was going to lose my mind. I though

Coming Out of the Rain

that I was going to die. I never thought that I would make it through. I had cried until I had no more tears left. I sacrificed, I went without, I was trying to live a Christian lift style, and I was tying to do what the Lord was telling me to do. But my world was still crumbling around me, it was being destroyed right before my very eyes, and it was taking me with it. There is a pain beyond compare that you feel in the depths of your soul, when you know that you are doing right, but everything in your life is still going wrong. My situation had gotten so bad, that I felt as though if one more thing went wrong in my life it was over for me.

But the one thing that I did not realize was whenever it rained hard it never lasted long, and it often ended as quickly as it started. When I was at my worst, the storm was just beginning to break. When the clouds began to roll away, and I could finally look up and see the sun beginning to burst through the dark clouds I knew then that my storm was passing by. That is when I began to realize that if I could hold on for just a little while longer everything would be all right. When I felt like this was it, and I could not take it anymore, that's when the Lord stepped in. Then I could finally realize what David meant when he said in Psalm 30:5:

Weeping may endure for a night but joy cometh in the morning.

He meant that no matter how bad it seemed it's only temporary. It is only going to rain as long as the Lord will allow it to. When we stop fighting the rain, and begin to embrace the rain the pain begins to cease. When we stop fighting the rain, and begin to allow the Lord to have total control over our lives, His divine plan for our existences becomes clear. I did not find true peace until I stopped fighting, and started excepting His will. In the beginning I could not understand why I was going through such a harsh storm, but now I realize that he did it for my good. Paul said in the book of Romans 8&28:

And we know that all things work together for good to them that love God, to them that are called according to his purpose.

All of my pain was for a purpose, and all of my heartaches were heaven sent. Everything that I went through in the storm made me a better man. I learned how to praise God in the midst of my trials, and in the midst of my tribulations. I learned that when everything was going wrong, and my world was being turned upside down I still had joy. Real Joy. The joy that the world couldn't give me, and the world couldn't take away. The day that I decided to

Coming Out of the Rain

take control of my storm was the day that I decided to live.

Chapter 8

Showers of The Anointing:

A New Beginning

After the resigning of the winds, and the ceasing of the rains, there's a new beginning. After the clouds have rolled away, and the sun has begun to shine again, it's a new day. And you must be very careful, for after having withstood your storm you can begin to feel as though you are almost invincible. You can begin to fell as though you can conquer anything, and whatever comes your way had better watch out because you are ready for a fight, and there is not a shadow of a doubt in your my that you can make it through. Because the very same problem that you thought would have killed you has been transformed into that which was needed in order to jumpstart your life. Now that the storm has passed you by you have acquired an undying sense of triumph, but you must realize that it was not you but the power that was working through you. Now you must be totally sure that you understand fully that this feeling of mastery is not based upon the fact that you were able to overcome your situations, but it was derived from the Anointing that you received while in the storm.

While the rain was falling, your anointing was being applied. The harder the rain fail, the heavier

Pastor Charles C. Brown

your anointing became. It is very important that you have a full understanding of what the anointing is. It is the authority and the power of God to overcome and destroy every yoke, and burden that the enemy has placed in your life. The things that you came up against in the spiritual realm were far too much for you to deal with while in the carnal or flesh sense. That is why the application of the anointing was so important because it was the anointing that overcame the spiritual wickedness that dwelt in high places. You must understand that the more you tried to fight the enemy using the flesh the weaker you became. It was not until after you had submitted yourself to the anointing of God did his power begin to flow through you. And the more you fought while under his authority, the easier the battle became. You have got to make the connection. The Bible say's in the book of Isaiah 10:27:

And it shall come to pass that day, that his burden (Satan) shall be taken away from off thy shoulder, and his yoke from thy neck, and the yoke shall be destroyed because of the anointing.

It was your anointing that brought you through, and broke the hold that the enemy had on your life. It was not your talents, your good looks, your money, your education, nor any of your abilities. It was the power of God that had enabled you to withstand the storm. When all of your planning had failed, and when all of your money had run out it was God that brought you through. After you had done all that you could do, and you still could not see how you were going to make it God stepped in right on time. And after you had finally begun to realize that only God could see you through, that was when the anointing took over.

Whenever you come into the presence of one of the saints of God who can stand up in a service, and just open their mouths and immediately you can feel the power of God that is the anointing. When before the preacher begins to speak a word, before a prayer is even uttered you already feel the presence of God that is the anointing. That is one thing that cannot be taught, nor can it be learned. It can only be applied in the storms of life. And if we are not careful we will look at these mighty warriors, and begin to say, "I wish that was me." We will even go as far as to say, "I wish that I could do that." Because the only thing that we can see is the end result, but what we cannot see is how they got to that point in their lives. What we can see is where they're at, but what we can't see is where they've been. You can see the benefits of the storm, but you can't see the sleepless nights, the missed meals, and the disappointments. You can't see the low points, the frustrations, and the lonely nights filled with tears. You can see the anointing at work, but you can't see the anointing being applied.

To anoint literally means to pour on, and when you anoint someone properly you must start at their head, and then allow the oil to flow downwards until it reaches their feet. When the prophet Samuel anointed David to be King over Israel, he raised the horn of oil over his head, and then, and only then did the oil begin to flow. The Bible say's in I Samuel 16&13:

Then Samuel took the horn of oil, and anointed him (David) in the midst of his brethren: and the spirit of the Lord came upon David from that day forward.

Coming Out of the Rain

After being anointed the spirit of God came upon him, and began to prepare him for his future. When you are truly anointed the spirit of God not only takes care of you today, but it will also take care of your tomorrow. The anointing of God begins to not only cover you, but it also over shadows you. When you have been through a severe storm, the anointing that is surrounding you is so strong that it can actually be felt whenever you enter a room. You don't have to say a word, and you don't have to pretend, or put on a show because the anointing will guide you, and lead you into the direction that the Lord our God would have you travel in. The Bible say's in Luke 12:11&12:

And when they bring you unto the synagogues, and unto magistrates, and powers, take ye no thought how or what thing ye shall answer, or what ye shall say: For the Holy Ghost shall teach you in the same hour what ye ought to say.

The anointing will guide you if you let it. In the midst of the storm the anointing was waiting for you to submit to it, but now that the storm is over the anointing is waiting for you to allow it to lead you. If you would allow the anointing to direct your path you will never find yourself in a situation that the Lord can not deliver you out of.

The anointing consecrates you. It makes you holy and acceptable unto the will of God. And when you become consecrated to God, He becomes devoted to protecting you from the powers of the enemy. Moses said in the book psalm 91:9-11:

Because thou hast made the Lord, which is my refuge, even the Most High, thy habitation; There shall no evil befall thee, neither shall any plague come nigh thy dwelling. For he shall give his angels charge over thee, to keep thee in all thy ways.

When you are consecrated you are dedicated to the Lord, and the Lord is dedicated to you. When the devil comes up in your life, the angels from Heaven go into battle. Then you are covered from the crown of your head to the soles of your feet, and the devil has no way of getting to you. When you are anointed you don't have to fight the battles, because the Lord will fight the battle for you. When the Lord is fighting the battle, the victory shall be yours. Then you can spend your time productively letting the world know that we serve a mighty God that sits high, and looks low. You can let the world know that there is a man from Galilee, who was born in a manger. That knew no sin, but became sin so that we would be freed from the bondages of sin. When the rain stops falling, and your new life begins you are drawn, or compelled by the power of the anointing to tell others about Christ. It becomes second nature. Because you know where you are, and you also know where you have been, and if you can help it you don't want anyone else to go through the hell that you've been through. You are compelled by the spirit of God to tell, everyone that you come into contact with about your new lease on life.

I have had my share of storms, and as I for stated in Chapter 7, there where times in my life when I did not know how I was going to make it through. But through the grace of God I made it, time after time He brought me out. But when I look back over my life, and evaluate my storms I can honestly say that, "The worst storm of all was being in love with someone that did not love me in return." I had found myself in a relationship with someone who no longer wanted to be in a relationship with me. That was the worst feeling that I had ever felt in my life. I thought that I could conquer anything, but this was a battle that I had no power over.

I thought that we would be together forever. I thought that we would never separate. I thought no one, and nothing could come in between us. I thought that the Lord our God himself had personally sent her into my life. I had prayed and prayed for a mate, and when my eyes fell upon her I thought that she was the answer to my prayers. That storm was so fierce, and I was so wrapped up in it that I thought I could not live without her. She was the air that I breathed, the purpose for my life, and I loved the very ground that she walked upon. I felt that a life without her would be a life that was not worth living. She was such a huge part of my life that I had grafted her into my future. When I made plans I made them for the both of us, because deep down within the very depths of my soul I knew that we would be together forever. I just knew it. I had prayed and prayed, and after my prayers were complete she walked into my life, and does not the Bible say in the book of Proverbs 18&22:

Whoso findeth a wife findeth a good thing, and obtaineth favor of the Lord.

Pastor Charles C. Brown

I thought that I had found my good thing, and that the favor of the Lord was shining upon my life. But what I had failed to realize, was the fact that even when you pray the lord is not going to answer your prayers until it is your time. And no matter how bad you feel that you must help God's plan for your life come to past, you must learn how to stand still and be patient because God does not need your help. I did not realize it then, but I do understand it now. For while I was in the midst of the storm the Lord was preparing me to receive my true wife, but I did not have patience and I fell for on of the oldest tricks in the book. For in the midst of everything that was going on in my life the devil had sent me a carbon copy of a good original in hopes of making me lose my blessings, and I fell for it hook, line, and sinker. In the midst of the rain instead of holding fast unto the hand of the Lord, I had grasped hold of the first piece of driftwood that passed by, and instead of taking me out of the storm, I was being dragged deeper and deeper into the raging waters.

It's funny how many times we can actually know that something is not right for us, but in an effort to make it seem right we begin to make up excuses. We begin to try to help God's hand move quicker, but instead of making it better we end up causing ourselves more pain and suffering. When men are tried of being alone, we tend to settle for the first tight skirt that passes by. And instead of getting someone that is good for us and to us, we end up getting someone that couldn't care less about us. We end up with a house built with bricks of sorrow and pain, and furnished with adultery, lying, cheating, and misery. And if we were to be totally honest with ourselves, nine times out of ten we usually end up in a worst state of being than when we started.

When women feel that their biological clocks are winding down, they tend to grab hold on to the first pair of jeans that happen to pass by. Not allowing their husbands to find them they go out and find a husband. Going against the very word of God, and still expecting the Lord to bless them. Instead of getting a man that is going to love, cherish, protect, and understand them for the rest of their lives they end up getting a boy that they will have to spend years trying to raise into a man.

God does not want his children to live their lives in that manner, he wants them to be able to enjoy the days of their lives with the one that they love, and with the one that is going to love them in return. When God made us He also made our perfect mates, but what we fail to do is wait for them to come. If we would only wait for our blessings it would save us a lot of time and energy that we wastefully spend in rebuilding our lives after we have allowed someone to come along and tare them down.

Pastor Charles C. Brown

In the midst of my storm, when God was preparing me for my future I felt that he was not moving fast enough, I was tired, I wanted a change, and I wanted it now. I looked around and saw others walking happily along holding hands with the ones that they loved, and that is what I wanted. So I did what I thought was the right thing to do, I did just what the devil had wanted me to do. I had decided that I couldn't wait any longer, my patience had come to an end, and I had made up in my mind that the next woman that I meet will be the one that I chose to spend the rest of my life with. And in doing so I stepped out of my level of anointing, and into a world of trouble. But out of all of the hurt that I put myself through, and out of all of the pain that I caused in my own life the anointing was still working favorably in my behalf. For in the midst of the storm I learned how to love unconditionally. I learned how to open my heart completely, and how to accept me for me. I learned that I did not have to change the person that I was in order for others to love me. I learned that if I trusted in the Lord he would allow me to find my true soul mate. He would allow me to find the rib that was taking out of my side in order to create my wife, and before I walked down the aisle with another man's wife the Lord our God showed me the error of my ways. He delivered me, he redeemed me, and then He forgave.

The Lord or God gave me a second chance, He bestowed unto a beautiful wife, and He allowed me to have a wonderful family, and for that I am ever so grateful.

After the storm was over, the anointing that had showered down into my life had given me a new beginning. It washed away all of the pain that I had carried around for so long, and all of the hurt from my many failed relationships. The anointing had mended my broken heart, and now a heart that was once filled with grief was now filled with hope for a brighter tomorrow. I had stopped holding on to the blame for all of my past mistakes, and I had finally begun to accept life for what it really was. I began to realize that all of my past relationships were only lessons, and stepping-stones that were designed to take me to the level of spirituality in which the Lord had wanted me to achieve from the beginning. I had stopped looking at the doors in my life that had been closed, and I had finally decided to walk through the door that was now open. The Bible say's in 2 Corinthians 5:17:

Therefore if any man be in Christ, he is a new creature: old things are passed away; behold, all things are become new.

My storm had passed, and I had made it through. I had a new outlook on life, and I was ready for a

Pastor Charles C. Brown

new beginning. Now my life made sense, and I was ready to come out of the rain.

Printed in the United States
22334LVS00006B/10